Maritime Signal Flags! How Boats Speak to Each Other (Boats for Kids)

Children's Boats & Ships Books

Left Brain Kids

Educational Books for Children

You might wonder how vessels communicate with one another for safety and to share news.

In early times, ships communicated with each another by the crew shouting messages or by sending a small boat to bring the message. Lights and musical instruments were used, too.

Maritime signal flags are used at sea. They are know as the International Maritime Signal Flags. They are the means of communication between ships, or ships and the shore, even if there is no power for the radio.

The individual flags have specific letters and numbers. The different combinations of these flags have special meanings that the boat operators and crew learn and master.

Maritime flags are international signals and can be used in various methods. Each flag represents a letter of the alphabet. These are used at sea to spell out short messages.

A- Alpha- It signals that a diver is underwater. It is to warn other boats to keep clear.

B- Bravo- It signals that the ship is taking and discharging a dangerous cargo.

C- Charlie- It signals 'Yes'

D- Delta- This is to inform other vessels to keep clear because the ship is maneuvering with difficulty.

E- Echo- This is to signal other vessels that the concerned ship is altering its course to starboard.

F- Foxtrot- It means the ship is disabled and requests to communicate.

G- Golf- The ship requires a pilot.

H- Hotel- This is to signal that a pilot is onboard.

I-   India- This is to signal that the ship is altering course to port.

J- **Juliet- This is to signal fire and asks other ships to keep clear for the ship carries dangerous cargo.**

K- Kilo- This is to signal that the ship desires to communicate with the other ship.

L- Lima- This is to signal other vessels to stop instantly.

M- Mike- This signals that the ship is stopped. It is also commonly used to signal that a doctor is onboard.

N- November- It signals 'No'.

O- Oscar- This means 'man overboard'.

P- Papa- This signals that the ship is about to sail and that personnel have to return to the ship.

Q- Quebec- This signals a request for clearance to enter port.

R- Romeo- This signals that the ship has stopped. It signals other vessel to make their way past it.

S- Sierra- This is to signal that engines are going astern.

T- Tango- This signals other ships to keep clear.

U- Uniform- This signals 'you are running into danger'.

V- Victor- It signals that the ship requires assistance.

W- Whiskey- It means 'require medical assistance'.

X- X-ray- This means 'stop what you are doing and watch for more messages'.

Y- Yankee- This is to signal others that the concerned ship is dragging anchor.

Z- Zulu- This means 'require a tug'.

Kids, do you love to memorize code words and safety meanings? Put the flags and their meaning on flash cards and learn the quick and easy way.

CPSIA information can be obtained
at www.ICGtesting.com
Printed in the USA
LVHW06s0922290418
575298LV00004B/14/P